A lionfish

Aquariums

Jill Kalz

A⁺

Smart Apple Media

COPYRIGHT

🐚 Published by Smart Apple Media

1980 Lookout Drive, North Mankato, MN 56003

Designed by Rita Marshall

Copyright © 2002 Smart Apple Media. International copyright reserved in all countries. No part of this book may be reproduced in any form without written permission from the publisher.

Printed in the United States of America

🐚 Photographs by Sally McCrae Kuyper, Tom Myers

🐚 Library of Congress Cataloging-in-Publication Data

Kalz, Jill. Aquariums / by Jill Kalz. p. cm. — (Enclosed environments series)

Includes bibliographical references (p.).

🐚 ISBN 1-58340-104-0

1. Aquariums—Juvenile literature. [1. Aquariums. 2. Aquarium fishes. 3. Fishes. 4. Pets.] I. Title.

SF457.3 .K35 2001   639.34—dc21   00-051580

🐚 First Edition 9 8 7 6 5 4 3 2 1

Aquariums

What is an Aquarium?

Water bubbles. Two bright blue fish chase each other around a rock. Another hides. A cluster of tiny eggs starts to hatch. All of this can happen right in your own house. And you can watch it all without getting wet! **Aquariums** are clear containers, or tanks, that hold water, plants, and animals. They are usually rectangular and made of glass, but can also be plastic. They can be as small as a one-half gallon (1.9 l) fish bowl or as large as the four-story Giant Ocean Tank at the New

Some aquariums contain only one kind of fish

England Aquarium. That aquarium holds 180,000 gallons (681,300 l) of seawater! Sharks, sea turtles, and over five hundred other creatures live together there. Aquariums are filled with freshwater or saltwater. Most aquariums in people's homes are freshwater tanks because they are easier to maintain. An average freshwater aquarium holds about 20 gallons (76 l) of water. It may include a few plants, rocks, and, of course, fish. Some aquariums contain only one kind of fish, like guppies or angelfish. Others contain a collection of different kinds that all

"Aqua" is the Latin word for water.

share the same feeding needs. These are called community tanks. The bottom of the tank should be covered with about two inches (5 cm) of gravel. This holds plants in place.

Angelfish thrive in freshwater

A large school of goldfish

Plants are very important to a healthy aquarium. And not just because they look nice. They give fish a place to lay eggs or hide. They provide food and clean up fish waste. Most importantly, they add **oxygen** to the water.

The Importance of Oxygen

Fish need oxygen to live. They breathe by taking water in through their mouths. **Gills** on each side of their heads remove oxygen from the water. When the fish exhale through their gills, they release **carbon dioxide** back into the water. Plants need the carbon dioxide to live. It becomes a cycle: the

fish need the oxygen that the plants make, and the plants need

the carbon dioxide that the fish make. 🐚 Moving water

mixes more oxygen into the aquarium environment and helps

Plants provide oxygen

release harmful gases into the air. It also gives fish a little exercise to swim against water that is moving. Most aquariums use air pumps or **airstones** to keep the water moving. ✺ The right amount of air is just one part of a successful aquarium. The temperature of the water is also important. Sudden temperature changes can kill fish quickly. Underwater heaters help

Rectangular tanks give fish more room and allow more oxygen in the water.

keep temperatures constant. Freshwater aquariums are usually 72° to 79° F (22° to 26° C). If an aquarium is too hot, algae grow. Fast. Algae are tiny green plants. They are not harmful,

but they can coat the aquarium glass and make it difficult to

see inside. If an aquarium is kept too cold, fish can get sick.

A bubble-eyed goldfish

Even Fish Need Light

Aquariums also need light to keep fish and plants healthy. Indirect sun or artificial lights work best. Direct sun can raise the water temperature and hurt the fish. Many aquariums have special hoods or covers with built-in light bulbs. About eight to ten hours of light per day is plenty. Fish need dark resting time, too. Plants make their own food with the help of the sun. This process is called **photosynthesis**. But aquarium fish must rely on their owners to feed them. Most freshwater fish eat two small meals per day. Their diet

may include dry food flakes, live worms, or thawed shrimp.

Some fish may even nibble on aquarium plants as a snack.

Artificial lighting reveals a rainbow of colors

Aquarium Hazards

Overfeeding is one of the most common reasons aquariums fail. If fish are overfed, the extra food can rot. The water turns cloudy. Dead fish, algae, sick plants, and overcrowding are some of the other problems that can occur from too much food. 🐚 Aquariums must also be kept clean. Plants help because they use fish waste as fertilizer. Snails and scavenger fish, such as catfish, act like vacuum cleaners. They eat leftover food and algae. Aquarium owners help by scraping

Clean water is essential for a successful aquarium

algae off walls, changing the water, and removing waste. Most aquariums also have a filter, which water flows through to trap waste. 🐚 Aquarium owners often add special touches to their aquariums, such as rocks, wood, bits of pot-tery, or even ceramic castles, ships, and deep-sea divers! 🐚 But fish are the stars

"Age" tap water for a few days before using it in your aquarium.

of the aquarium. Neon blue, red, orange, striped, and spotted. Some are shy. Some are bullies. Some crawl along the bottom. Others come to the surface often. A well-balanced aquarium should have healthy fish swimming at every level. 🐚 All

aquariums share the same goal: to meet the needs of the plants

and animals living inside them. With everything in balance, a

well-designed aquarium is a work of art.

A spotted fish can be the star of an aquarium

Finding Air in Water

Fish need oxygen to survive. They use their gills to take oxygen out of the water. See how much oxygen is in a glass of plain water.

What You Need
A glass
Cold water
A warm, sunny window

What You Do
1. Fill a glass half full with cold water.
2. Set the glass in a sunny window for a couple of hours.

What You See
The tiny bubbles on the sides of the glass are air. You can add even more oxygen to the water by placing a straw in your glass and gently blowing on it. This is just what an air pump does.

A discus fish blends into its surroundings

INFORMATION

Index

Words to Know

airstones (AIR STONES)—stones with tiny holes through which air is pumped

algae (AL-jee)—very tiny green plants that live in water

aquariums (a-QUAIR-ee-ums)—water-filled containers that hold plants and animals

carbon dioxide (CAR-bun die-OX-eyed)—a gas released by animals during breathing

gills (GILLZ)—breathing organs that help animals obtain oxygen from water

oxygen (OK-si-jen)—a gas needed to keep plants and animals alive

photosynthesis (fo-to-SIN-the-sis)—the process of changing the energy of sunlight into food

tanks (TANGKS)—large containers for liquids or gases

Read More

Evans, Mark, adapted by Roger A. Caras. *ASPCA Pet Care Guides for Kids: Fish.* New York: DK Publishing, Inc., 1993.

Landau, Elaine. *Your Pet Tropical Fish.* New York: Children's Press, 1998.

Mills, Dick. *You and Your Aquarium.* New York: Alfred A. Knopf, 1986.

Morley, Christine, and Carole Orbell. *Me and My Pet Fish.* Chicago: World Book, Inc., 1997.

Internet Sites

AquaLink
http://www.aqualink.com/

Aquaria Central ·
http://www.aquariacentral.com/

Fish Link Central
http://www.fishlinkcentral.com/

Monterey Bay Aquarium
http://www.mbayaq.org/